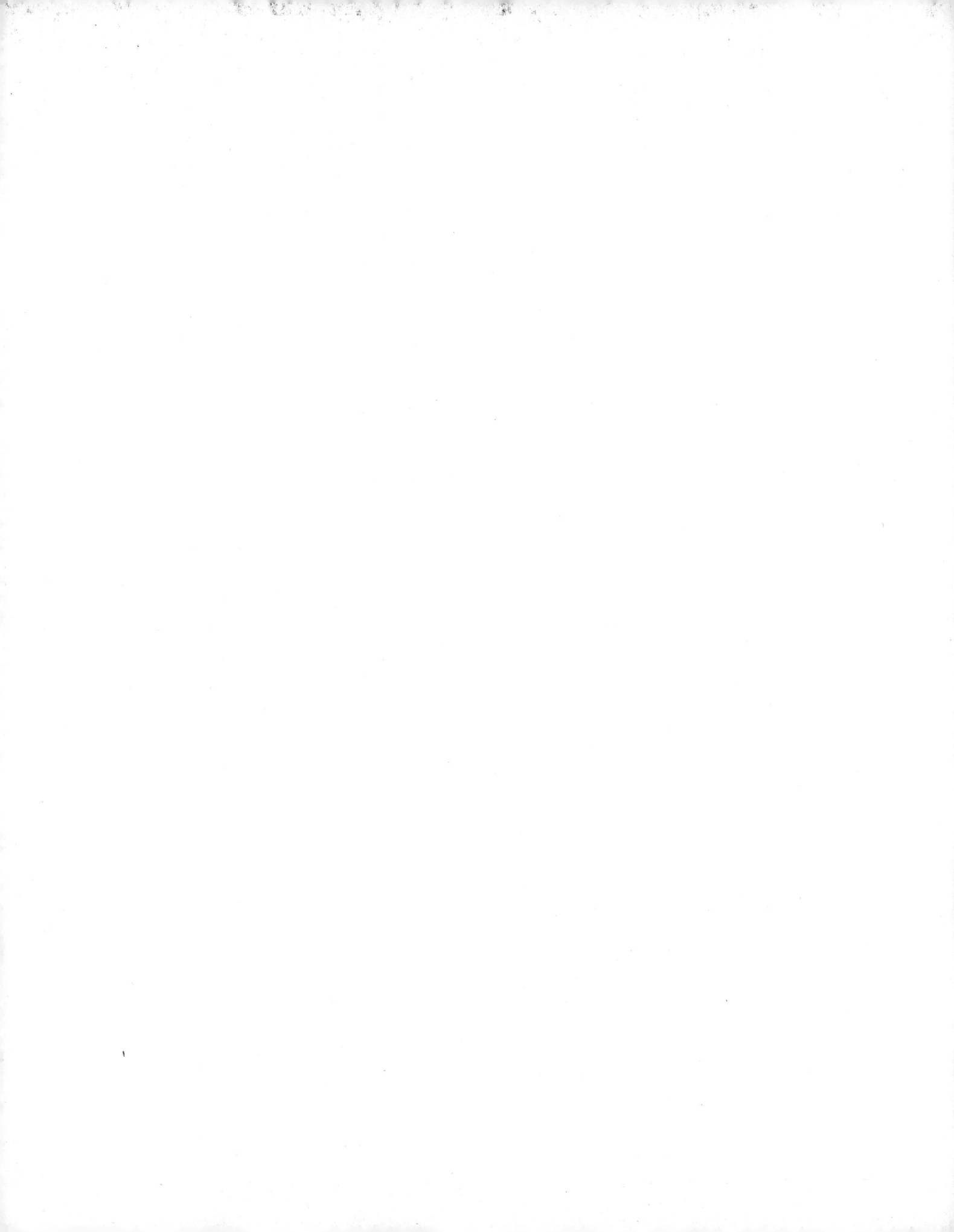

What's special to me?

Religious Books

Anita Ganeri

W
HODDER
Wayland

an imprint of Hodder Children's Books

Contents

All Wayland books encourage children to read and help them improve their literacy.

✓ The contents page, page numbers, headings and index help to locate a particular piece of information.

✓ The glossary reinforces alphabetic knowledge and extends vocabulary.

✓ The books to read section suggests other books dealing with the same subject.

Special Books

Do you have a favourite book? Why is it so special to you? Perhaps you like reading the story best or looking at the pictures.

Religions also have special books called holy or sacred books. They help to teach people how to live their lives in a good way.

Hindu Holy Books

Hindus have many different holy books. These Hindus in India are visiting a **mandir** where they listen to readings from the holy books. The holy books teach Hindus how to live and worship in the right way.

The Hindu holy books were first spoken and then written down in Sanskrit, a very ancient Indian language. The oldest books are called the **Vedas** and the **Upanishads**. Many of the Hindu texts include hymns to praise the gods.

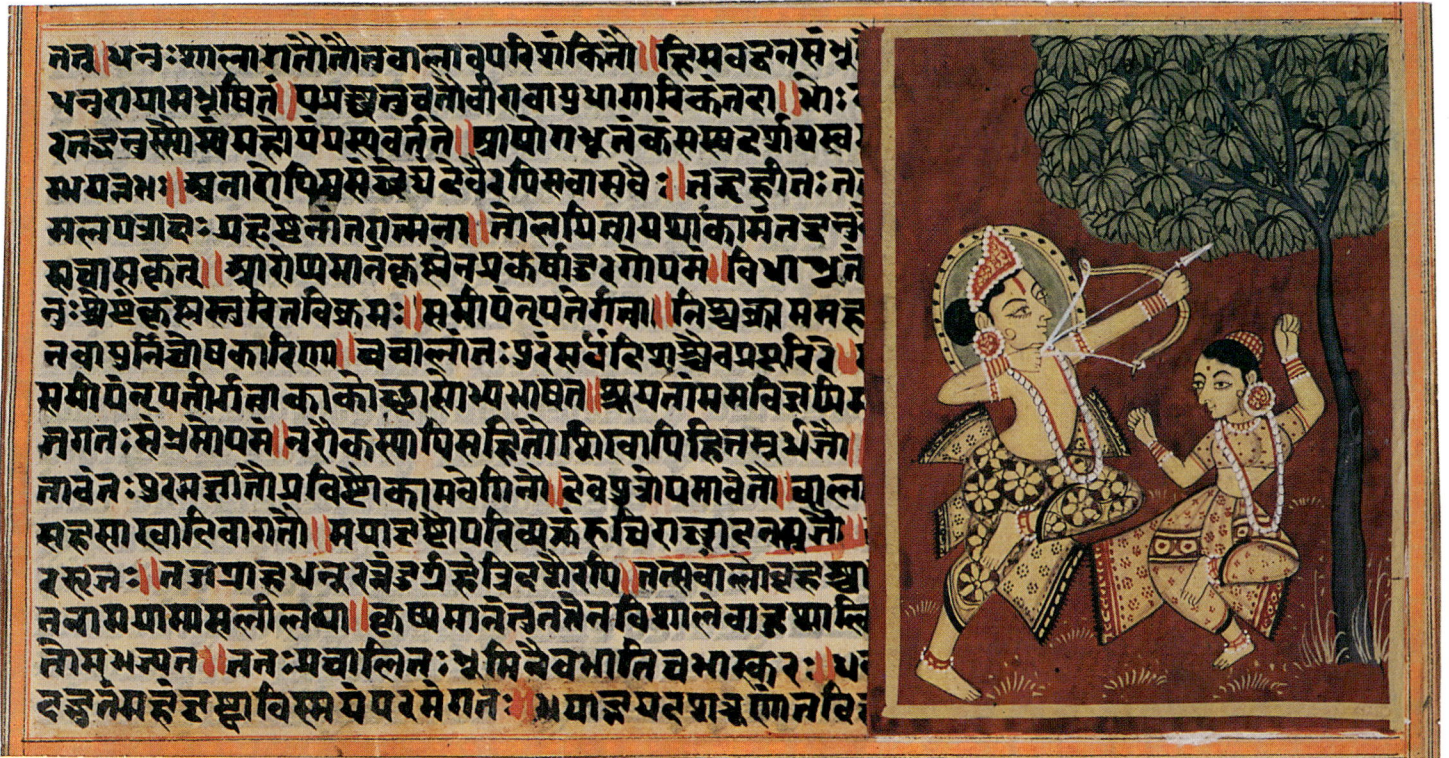

This page is from the Ramayana, a poem which tells the story of the god **Rama** and his wife, Sita.

In the story, Rama, the heir to the throne, is sent away to live in a forest. His wife Sita is kidnapped by the demon Ravana. Rama rescues her and kills the demon. This story shows how good wins over evil.

Another poem is from the **Bhagavad Gita**.
It is the story of a war between two royal
families. The god **Krishna** is the **charioteer**
of Prince Arjuna. He teaches the prince that
he must do his duty without thinking about
himself. This is very important for Hindus.

7

The Torah

The name Torah means the 'Books of Teaching'. It is the first and holiest part of the Tenakh or Jewish Bible. Jewish people believe that the book shows them how God wants them to live.

Jews believe that God gave the Torah to Moses on Mount Sinai, more than 3,000 years ago. Moses was the leader chosen by God. Jews believe he brought back the **Ten Commandment**s, carved on stone tablets.

Jews read the Torah from **scrolls** of parchment, which are kept in a special cupboard in the **synagogue**. This cupboard is called the Ark. The scrolls are wrapped in beautiful cloths called mantles.

The scrolls are taken out of the Ark for reading. The reader follows the words with a silver pointer because the scrolls are too precious to touch. The Torah is written in the **Hebrew** language.

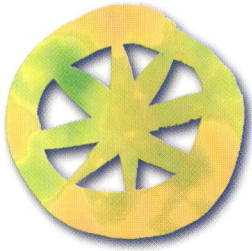

Special Buddhist Books

Buddhists have many special books. Some tell stories about the life of the Buddha, who lived 2,500 years ago in India. Others give the Buddha's teachings, which Buddhists try to follow as their guide.

This Buddhist **monk** is reading and studying a holy book. The Buddha taught people to be kind, generous and honest and not to hurt living things. Buddhists also chant parts of the books out loud. Chanting means that you half-sing, half-speak the words.

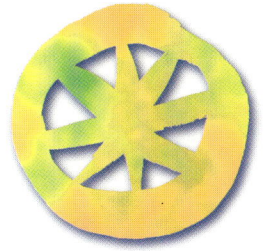

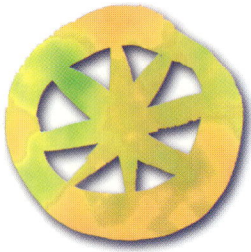

The Buddha's teachings were written down by monks. In some **monasteries**, monks still make books using skills that are hundreds of years old. Copying the texts is very hard work but is a way of showing great respect for the Buddha.

Some Buddhist texts are written in ancient Indian languages. One book is called the Pali Canon, or Three Baskets, meaning that the texts are in three sections. Some Buddhists think that the third Basket is the best record of the Buddha's teaching.

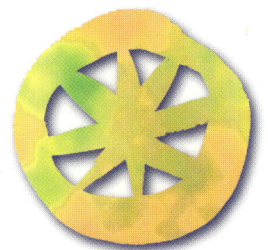

The Bible

The Christian holy book is the Bible. It is divided into the Old Testament and the New Testament. The New Testament tells the story of Jesus's life. Christians believe that Jesus was the son of God.

Parts of the Bible are read at church
services. Reading the Bible tells Christians
about God and helps them to understand
how God wants them to live. This is why
the Bible is so special.

In church, Christians praise God with hymns and prayers which are taken from the Bible. These include special poems called Psalms that come from the Old Testament.

Many Christians read the Bible every day on their own. It teaches them about God's love for the world and how to live their lives. If they are sad, many Christians find that reading the Bible can help them to feel better.

The Qur'an

The Qur'an is the Muslim holy book. Muslims believe that it is the word of **Allah**. Allah gave the words of the Qur'an to the Prophet Muhammad (ﷺ) who passed them on to his followers.

Copies of the Qur'an are very precious and are treated with great respect. Muslims prepare themselves by washing their hands and feet before they touch or read from the holy book.

The Qur'an is written in Arabic. Many Muslim children learn to read Arabic at a special school in the **mosque** so that they can read the Qur'an for themselves.

Muslims learn verses from the Qur'an by heart and use them in their daily prayers. They believe that the Qur'an is a message from Allah. It tells them how Allah wishes them to live and worship.

The Guru Granth Sahib

For Sikhs, the Guru Granth Sahib is a special book because it guides them in their lives. It was put together by a Sikh **guru**. It is made up of hymns written by Sikh teachers and holy men. It has the message that people should love God.

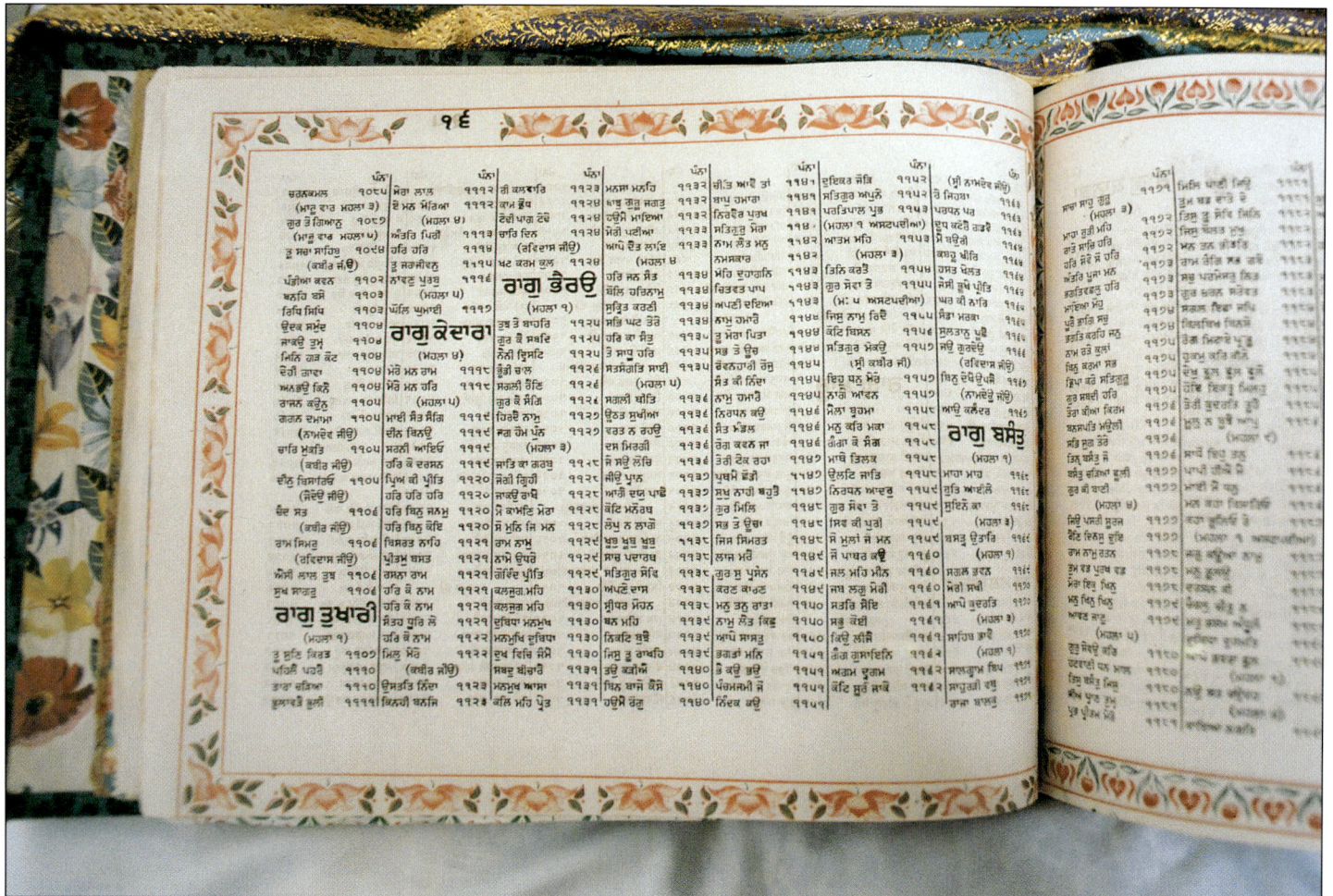

The Guru Granth Sahib is used in all Sikh worship in the **gurdwara**. A man or woman called a granthi reads from the book and looks after it. At festivals, the Guru Granth Sahib is read right through from beginning to end.

The Guru Granth Sahib is the most precious thing in the gurdwara. It is placed on a throne, like a king, to show how special it is. A fan is waved over it to show respect. When it is not being read, the Guru Granth Sahib is wrapped in fine silk cloth.

Sikhs treat the Guru Granth Sahib with great respect because it tells them about God. When Sikhs go into the gurdwara, they bow or kneel in front of it and give offerings of money, flowers and food.

Notes for teachers

Pages 4 & 5 Hindu scriptures are divided into two broad groups, shruti (or 'revealed') and smriti (or 'remembered'). The earliest texts are the Vedas, meaning knowledge or wisdom. These were composed some 3,000 years ago. They were not written down but memorized and passed down orally from teacher to pupil. Hindus listen to readings at at a mandir or temple.The shruti texts are so-called because they are believed to have been 'revealed' by Brahma, the creator, to certain holy men. The four Vedas are collections of hymns in praise of the gods and instructions for conducting rituals. The most important and oldest is the Rig Veda. It contains over a thousand hymns, including the Gayatri Mantra in praise of the Sun god which Hindus use in daily worship. The Vedas and Upanishads were spoken, then written, in Sanskrit, an ancient Indo-European language. The word 'Sanskrit' means 'perfected'. It was believed that people could communicate with the gods in Sanskrit, but only if they recited the words perfectly.

Pages 6 & 7 Smriti texts include the two great Hindu epic poems, the Ramayana and the Mahabharata. The Ramayana tells the story of Rama and Sita. Rama is a great hero, a loyal friend and heir to the throne who becomes a wise and just king. In short, he is a model human being. The moral of the story is the constant struggle between good and evil in the world, with good ultimately victorious. The Mahabharata tells of a war between two rival, and closely related, royal families, the Kauravas and Pandavas.

The Bhagavad Gita is the most important part of the Mahabharata. It is set on the battlefield, on the eve of battle. Krisha reminds Arjuna, a Pandava prince, that it is his moral duty to fight, even against his cousins. He must do his duty without thought of himself. Both stories are hugely popular. They are communicated through dance, drama, books, children's comic strips and even as serials on Indian television. Both Rama and Krishna are avatars (incarnations) of the god Vishnu.

Pages 8 & 9 The Torah is the first part of the Tenakh, the Jewish Bible. It contains the five Books of Teaching which God gave to Moses on Mount Sinai. The Tenakh is made up of 24 books, divided into three parts – the Books of Teaching (Torah); the Books of Prophets (Nevi'im) and the Books of Writings (Ketuvim). Their initial letters, T, N and KH, form the word Tenakh. Other Jewish holy books include the Talmud, a collection of laws and commentaries, and prayer books, such as the Haggadah which contains the prayers, service and songs for the Seder night, celebrated at the start of Pesach. Jews believe that almost two months after Moses led the Jews out of Egypt, God chose them to receive the Torah. The stone tablets on which the Ten Commandments were written were kept in a golden chest called the Ark of the Covenant. It was later taken to Jerusalem where it was installed in the Holy of Holies, the inner sanctum of the Temple.

Pages 10 & 11 The Torah scrolls are handwritten on parchment by highly skilled scribes and according to strict rules. The Torah is read in the synagogue at weekly Shabbat prayers, and on special occasions such as festivals and rites of passage, such as a boy's Bar Mitzvah or a girl's Bat Mitzvah. Each of the five books is divided into sections called sidrot, making 54 sidrot altogether. At least one section is read every Shabbat so that one whole cycle of readings is completed each year. This is marked by a celebration called Simchat Torah, 'the rejoicing in the Torah'. The Torah scrolls are taken out of the Ark and carried in a procession around the synagogue or outdoors.

Pages 12 & 13 For about 400 years after his death, the Buddha's teachings were memorized and passed on orally, by chanting, by Buddhist monks. Two councils were called in the 4th century BCE to collate the teachings and agree on a definitive version of the Buddha's message. At the second council, differences of opinion arose as to what the Buddha actually taught. This division led to the emergence of the two main schools of Buddhism – Theravada and Mahayana. Theravada Buddhists took as their scriptures texts which could be traced back, historically, to the Buddha. Mahayana Buddhists believed that other teachings were also important. Theravada scriptures are written in Pali, an ancient, colloquial Indian language, spoken by the Buddha. Mahayana scriptures are written in Sanskrit.

Pages 14 & 15 The first Buddhist texts to be written down became known as the Pali Canon or Tipitaka. They are the sacred texts of the Theravada Buddhists. Tipitaka means 'Three Baskets', possibly after the baskets in which the palm leaves used instead of paper in book-making, were stored. The first 'basket' or section is the Vinaya Pitaka, which contains the rules the monks or nuns should follow.

The second basket, the Sutta Pitaka, contains the Buddha's teachings. It includes the Dhammapada, a very popular collection of the Buddha's sayings. The third basket, the Abhidamma Pitaka, contains philosophical and doctrinal arguments. Passages from the sacred texts are recited during puja (Buddhist worship). Buddhist monks spend a great deal of their time studying and discussing the texts and explaining their meaning to devotees. The texts are chanted as part of meditation.

Pages 16 & 17 For Christians, the Bible is the revelation of God's relationship with human beings. Despite being given the guidance of laws, teachings and prophets, people fell into sin, or wrong doing, which separated them from God. The New Testament shows how God came to Earth as Jesus Christ, and through Jesus's life, death and resurrection repaired this relationship and brought people closer to God again. The New Testament is, therefore, of particular importance to Christians because it includes descriptions of Jesus's life and ministry (the Gospels), as well as writings by the early Christians (the Epistles). It provides Christians with an authoritative guide as to how to live their lives although different groups of Christians have different ways of interpreting the Bible's guidance and inspiration.

Pages 18 & 19 The Christian Old Testament corresponds to the Jewish Bible. Roman Catholic and Orthodox Bibles also include other books and parts of books, known as the Apocrypha in the Old Testament. These are not part of Protestant Bibles. The Old Testament tells of the creation of the world, the history of the early Jews and the covenant which God made with Abraham. It teaches that salvation comes through obeying God's laws. The New Testament teaches that salvation comes through belief in Jesus Christ and in following his example. The gospels were written about 70-150 years after Jesus's death by the four evangelists, Matthew, Mark, Luke and John. Gospel means good news. The Epistles (letters) were written about 30 years after Jesus's death, mostly by a Jew called Saul who converted to Christianity and changed his name to Paul after seeing a vision of Christ.

Pages 20 & 21 Muslims believe that the words of the Qur'an were revealed to the Prophet Muhammad (ﷺ) by Allah through the Angel Jibril. The revelations began in about 610 CE and ended shortly before Muhammad's death. Muhammad could not read or write so he learnt the words off by heart and recited them to his followers. They later wrote them down to form the Qur'an. The Qur'an is divided into 114 verses, called surahs. Apart from surah 9, all begin with the same words, 'In the name of Allah, most gracious, most merciful'. Some surahs give instructions about how Muslims should behave and worship, such as the times of daily prayers, fasting at Ramadan, the giving of charity and the importance of loving and obeying Allah. Together with the Sunnah (the way of life shown by Muhammad through his sayings, thoughts and actions), the Qur'an is the basis of the Shari'ah or holy law.

Pages 22 & 23 Because it is believed to come directly from Allah, the Qur'an can never be changed. The version used today has remained unaltered since about 30 years after Muhammad's death in 632 CE. For worship, it is always read in Arabic, the most sacred language for Muslims because it was the language chosen by Allah to reveal his wishes for the world. Even Muslims who are not Arabic speakers learn to recite verses from the Qur'an.

The word Qur'an means 'reading' or 'recitation' and learning to read and recite from the Qur'an is considered an important means of paying respect. Some Muslims learn the whole Qur'an by heart and are given the title 'hafiz'.

Pages 24 & 25 Just before his death in 1708, the tenth Sikh guru, Guru Gobind Singh, decreed that there would be no more human gurus after him. Instead, Sikhs should turn to the Guru Granth Sahib for guidance. So the Guru Granth Sahib became the Sikhs' teacher. It had been called the Adi Granth, or first book. Its new name reflected its new role. Granth means 'book'. Sahib is a term of respect. Any building in which a Guru Granth Sahib is installed becomes a gurdwara. The Guru Granth Sahib is used in all forms of Sikh worship, including festivals, naming ceremonies and weddings. A baby's name is chosen by opening the Guru Granth Sahib at random and taking the first letter of the first word on the left-hand page. This letter begins the baby's name. The scriptures are ceremonially 'put to bed' at night in a separate room and returned to the worship room in the morning.

Pages 26 & 27 The Guru Granth Sahib consists of 1,430 pages. Each copy has exactly the same page length and numbering. So a hymn in one copy can always be found in exactly the same place in another. It is written in the sacred Gurmukhi script, the alphabet used to write the Punjabi language. Gurmukhi means 'from the mouth of the Guru'. Gurmukhi classes are held in many gurdwaras in Britain. Sikhs treat the Guru Granth Sahib with the same devotion that would be shown to a human guru. During a reading, a chauri, or ceremonial fan made of horse or yak hair in a silver or wooden handle, is waved over it. In India, this was a traditional sign of respect shown to gods and kings. The message of the Guru Granth Sahib is that salvation does not depend on caste or other divisions but on constant love and service of God.

Glossary

Allah The Muslim word for God.

Bhagavad Gita One of the Hindu holy books. It tells the story of Krishna and Prince Arjuna.

charioteer A person who drives a chariot (wheeled cart).

gurdwara A place where Sikhs go to worship.

guru A great Sikh teacher or leader.

Hebrew The holy language of the Jews.

Krishna The name of a popular Hindu god. He is the hero of the Bhagavad Gita.

mandir A place where Hindus go to worship.

monasteries Places where monks live, work and worship.

monk A holy man who lives a very simple, strict life.

mosque A Muslim holy building.

Rama The name of a popular Hindu god. He is the hero of the Ramayana.

scrolls Rolls of paper or parchment on which the Jewish holy texts are written.

synagogue A place where Jews go to worship.

Ten Commandments God's laws, as given to Moses on Mount Sinai.

Upanishads and **Vedas** Very ancient collections of Hindu holy books.

Books to read

HINDU
Celebrate Hindu Festivals by Dilip Kadodwala and Paul Gateshill (Heinemann, 1995)

The Elephant-Headed God and other Hindu Tales by Debjani Chatterjee (Lutterworth, 1989)

JEWISH
Sofer: the Story of a Torah Scroll by Eric Ray (Aura Productions, 1986)

BUDDHIST
The Birth of the Buddha by Owen Cole and Judith Lowndes (Heinemann, 1995)

Jakata Tales by Abbie Blum and Lynn Dremalas (Dharma Publishing, 1992)

CHRISTIAN
The Beginner's Bible by Karyn Henley (Kingsway Productions, 1989)

The Bible by Lois Rock (Lion Publishing, 1994)

SIKH
Sikh by Jenny Wood (Watts, 1998)

GENERAL SERIES ON RELIGION:
Beliefs and Cultures series (Franklin Watts, 1997/8)
Everyday Religion series (Wayland, 1996/7)
Introducing Religions series (Heinemann, 1997)
Looking at Christianity series and **Looking at Judaism** series (Wayland, 1998)

Editor: Sarah Doughty
Design: Sterling Associates
Consultant: Alison Seaman

First published in Great Britain in 1998 by Wayland (Publishers) Ltd
Reprinted in 2000 by Hodder Wayland, an imprint of Hodder Children's Books

© Hodder Wayland 1998

Hodder Children's Books, a division of Hodder Headline, 338 Euston Road, London NW1 3BH

British Library Cataloguing in Publication Data
Ganeri, Anita
    Religious books. - (What's Special to me?)
    1. Sacred books - Juvenile literature
    I. Title
    291.8'2

ISBN 0 7502 2242 5

Printed and bound by G. Canale & C.S.p.A., Turin

Picture Acknowledgements: Bipinchandra J. Mistry 6; Circa Photo Library (Barrie Searle) title page, 5, 7, (Barrie Searle) 8, 10, (Barrie Searle) 10, 20 (left), (John Smith) 24; Getty Images (Nabeel Turner) 22; Sally and Richard Greenhill Photo Library (Richard Greenhill) 27; Robert Harding 9, 12, 15; Christine Osborne Pictures 4, 17, 18, 21, 25 (left and right), 26; Peter Sanders cover (left) 23; Trip (T Bognar) 13, (B Vikander) 14, (H Rogers) 16; Wayland Picture Library (Jenny Woodcock) cover, 3, (Jenny Woodcock) 19; Zefa 11, 20 (right).

Index

Entries in **bold** are pictures